D1484885

Photo by Ken Huth

Set design by G.W. Mercier

Jeff Gurner, Heather Ayers and John Bolton in a scene from the Geva Theatre Center production of *Five Course Love*.

FIVE COURSE LOVE

BOOK, MUSIC AND LYRICS BY
GREGG COFFIN

DRAMATISTS
PLAY SERVICE
INC.

FIVE COURSE LOVE
Copyright © 2007, Gregg Coffin

All Rights Reserved

SPECIAL NOTE

FIVE COURSE LOVE
Book, Music & Lyrics by Gregg Coffin

AUTHOR'S NOTE

FIVE COURSE LOVE is a vaudeville. Think sketch comedy and you're think-ing right. Rent every episode you can find of *Your Show of Shows* and *The Carol Burnett Show*. Watch *Looney Tunes* cartoons. Eat food while you're doing all of that, and you'll know what to do with FIVE COURSE LOVE.

The curtain speech is MANDATORY, and it is to be performed as a voiceover, not LIVE. You can use my recording (included with the complete set of scores) or record your own (sheet music is provided as the first song in the score). It tells the audience from Square One that it is OK to laugh at this show. And laugh at low humor and low rhymes.

Don't cure polio with this piece. Don't end wars. Just make a couple hundred people forget about their troubles for ninety minutes, and revel in the talents of three character actors as they go through their paces as fast as they possibly can.

Bon Appetit.

—Gregg

FIVE COURSE LOVE was produced by Geva Theatre Center (Mark Cuddy, Artistic Director; John Quinlivan, Managing Director) and Five Course Love LLC at the Minetta Lane Theatre in New York City, opening on October 16, 2005. It was directed by Emma Griffin; the set and costume design were by G.W. Mercier; the lighting design was by Mark Barton; the choreography was by Mindy Cooper; the sound design was by Rob Kaplowitz; the dramaturg was Marge Betley; and the musical direction was by Fred Tessler; the offstage singers were Erin Maguire and Billy Sharpe; the musicians were Fred Tessler (conductor/keyboards), Carl Haan (keyboards), Taylor Price (guitar/bass) and Steve McKeown (percussion). The cast was as follows:

BARBIE, SOFIA, GRETCHEN, ROSALINDA, KITTY .... Heather Ayers
MATT, GINO, KLAUS, GUILLERMO, CLUTCH .... John Bolton
DEAN, CARLO, HEIMLICH, ERNESTO, POPS .... Jeff Gurner

CHARACTERS

Actor 1
MATT, GINO, KLAUS, GUILLERMO, CLUTCH

Actor 2
BARBIE, SOFIA, GRETCHEN, ROSALINDA, KITTY

Actor 3
DEAN, CARLO, HEIMLICH, ERNESTO, POPS

SETTINGS

Matt's car

Dean's Old-Fashioned All-American Down-Home Bar-B-Que Texas Eats

La Trattoria Pericolo

Der Schlupfwinkel Speiseplatz

Ernesto's Cantina

The Star-Lite Diner

"If music be the food of love, play on."

—*Shakespeare*

"Ce qui ne vaut pas la peine d'etre dit, on le chant."

—*Beaumarchais*

FIVE COURSE LOVE

At "places," and with the audience seated, the following voiceover announcement is heard …

VOICEOVER. Ladies and gentlemen, the Five Course Love Choral Society with a brief message regarding this production.
WELCOME TO *FIVE COURSE LOVE*
WE HOPE YOU ALL ENJOY THE SHOW
BUT FIRST SOME BRIEF REMINDERS
WE WANTED YOU TO KNOW
BY ORDER OF THE FIRE MARSHALL,
FOLKS, THIS GUY'S NOT KIDDING,
TAKE A MOMENT TO FIND
THE NEAREST EMERGENCY EXIT FROM WHERE YOU'RE SITTING
WE PROMISE NO ONE SMOKES ONSTAGE
THEY SING, THEY'RE ALL BIG BREATHERS
AND UNLESS YOU'VE BEEN LIVING IN A CAVE
YOU KNOW THAT YOU CAN'T LIGHT UP EITHER
PLEASE FOLKS, NO PHOTOGRAPHY
NO RECORDING, 'CUZ IF YOU DO
SOME BIG AND BURLY USHER WILL BEAT
THE *(A bleep.)* RIGHT OUT OF YOU
AND FINALLY, THERE'S A FIERY PIT
WHERE WE WILL SURELY FLING
ALL THOSE THEATRE PATRONS
WHOSE CELL PHONES START TO RING *(Cell phones ringing.)*
SO TURN 'EM OFF NOW, SIT BACK
AND THINK OF ALL THE STARS ABOVE
NOW, CUE THE PIT *(A note from the band.)*
DIM THESE LIGHTS A BIT *(House lights dim.)*
'CUZ HERE COMES *FIVE COURSE LOVE.*

(Blackout and we hear a short overture followed by a cacophony of car horns, not deafening but certainly insistent. Then a lone voice rises above the traffic and shouts ...)

MATT. Any particular SHADE of green you're waiting for?! Let's gooooooooooooo!
(Lights up immediately on Matt in his car. He is pocket-protectored and horn-rimmed, and stuck in traffic on the way to his first date in a very long time.)

WHY THE HELL THE TRAFFIC?
WHY THE HELL THE WAIT?
AND WHY'D IT HAVE TO HAPPEN
ON THE NIGHT I LAND THIS DATE?
I'VE COUNTED DOWN THE DAYS UNTIL THIS MINUTE,
FOR A CHANCE TO HAVE ONE NIGHT WITH SOME GIRL IN IT!
(To the driver in front of him.) Come ONNN!!!
'CUZ I AM NOT A WINNER.
NOPE. I DON'T EVEN PLACE.
A WOMAN'S INTUITION
GOES NO FURTHER THAN THIS FACE.
SOME PHEROMONE, SOME "TURN-AND-RUN" AROMA
IS KEEPING MY LIBIDO IN A COMA!
I AM A VERY SINGLE MAN.
A VERY SINGLE MAN.
WHO IS TRYING THE BEST HE CAN.
I'VE GOT A BIG BOUQUET
(He shows us some flowers that are sitting on the car seat.)
AND SOME "BREATH-AWAY"
(He sprays some in his mouth.)
A LITTLE RENDEZVOUS
A LITTLE TABLE FOR TWO.
A COUPLE SALADS TOSSED,
A COUPLE FINGERS CROSSED.
(To the driver.) JUST DRIVE! Put the phone down ... and DRIVE!!!
PALMS ARE GETTING CLAMMY.
A SWEAT BEGINS TO BREAK.
AND NONE OF THIS RESEMBLES
THE EFFECT I'D LIKE TO MAKE.
CARY GRANT OR HUMPHREY BOGART,
STEVE McQUEEN, PLEASE!
(Checking his hair and sweating brow in the rearview.)
NOT STUCK IN TRAFFIC
AS THE RED CHANGES TO GREEN, PLEASE!

(To the driver.) Move … your … *(Car horn as he mouths "Ass!")*
>TRIED A DATING SERVICE,
>'CUZ I WAS RUNNING OUT OF ROPE.
>SKEPTICAL AND NERVOUS
>BUT THEY SAID, "DON'T GIVE UP HOPE."
>THEN YESTERDAY THEY FORWARDED AN EMAIL!
>SUBJECT: "GREETINGS FROM A VERY SINGLE FEMALE!"
>AND I'M A VERY SINGLE MAN!

(Then notices he's being watched by another driver, quietly.)
>A VERY SINGLE MAN … *(Giving the driver "the finger.")*
>WHO IS TRYING THE BEST HE CAN
>TO BE A MORE PLURAL BOY,
>PLURAL LIKE A BOY WITH A "GIR-RUL" BOY.
>AND HERE'S THE PLACE
>AND A PARKING SPACE,
>AND A MINUTE TO SPARE
>SO CHECK THE HAIR
>AND PRAY!
>ST. VALENTINE, WAY UP THERE IN YOUR HEAVEN
>I COULD REALLY USE A HAND DOWN HERE,
>FROM EIGHT UNTIL ELEVEN.
>IF YOU'VE GOT PLANS TONIGHT
>PLEASE SEND REGRETS, I'VE EARNED THE RIGHT
>I'M A DIRE CASE
>I NEED HELP FROM A HIGHER PLACE.
>HEY CUPID, PLEASE, I'M SEEKING SANCTUARY
>GIVE ME ONE NIGHT THAT DOESN'T END SO SOLITARY.
>PLEASE SHIELD THIS SUSHI BAR FROM ANY ADVERSARY.
>SEND YOUR HELP BELOW.
>'CUZ HERE I GO.

(Intoned.) In-The-Name-Of-The-Father-And-The-Son-And-The-Holy-Ghost-May-The-Force-Be-With-Me-Let's-Win-One-For-The-Gipper … Say … this doesn't look like The Samurai Sushi Palace to ME! *(And he's right. This is not the Samurai Sushi Palace; instead it's a rib joint called Dean's Old Fashioned All-American down-home Bar-B-Que Texas Eats. Texas swing music begins. Dean, the owner and host, enters in full country regalia, shouting out to an unseen table and waitress.)*

DEAN. Rhonda Sue, I need a pitcher and a half-rack at Table Seven … PRONTO!!!

MATT.
>AH, EXCUSE ME. WHERE'D THE SUSHI GO?

DEAN.

    BUTCH, THEY BROKE CAMP TWO MONTHS AGO.

    PACKED IT ALL UP, AND WASABI-ED ON OUTTA HERE.

MATT. Great!

DEAN.

    ARE YOU MEETING SOMEONE? HELL, YOU LOOK LIKE YOU ARE.

    HEY, PROB'LY THAT ROSEBUD WAITIN' AT THE BAR.

    SHE ASKED ME TO KEEP MY EYES PEELED. YOU NEED A BEER?

MATT. No, thanks.

DEAN.

    BUTCH! YOU GOTTA GET INTO THE SWING O' THINGS,

    'CUZ THAT AIN'T HOW THIS RIB JOINT SINGS.

    COME ON NOW, TAKE THE STICK OUT. SIT A SPELL!

    BUTCH! I'M GONNA TELL YOU SOMETHING, AND IT'S GONNA
      BE BLUNT.

    BETTER LOOSEN UP 'CUZ THIS DOG WON'T HUNT.

    TONIGHT YOU'RE RINGIN' A REAL LIVE SOUTHERN BELLE.

    HERE AT DEAN'S OLD-FASHIONED ALL-AMERICAN

    DOWN-HOME BAR-B-QUE TEXAS EATS.

    WHERE THE BEER'S ICE COLD AND THE CHILI'S RED HOT

    AND THE JUKEBOX CAN'T BE BEAT!

    WE'VE GOT RIBS AND STEAKS IN HICK'RY SAUCE

    WE'VE GOT CORNBREAD, PIE AND MORE.

    AND BUTCH, I'D TELL YOU THE SPECIALS, SON …

    BUT WE MIGHT HAVE TO …

    WE MIGHT HAVE TO PEEL YOU OFF THE FLOOR, BUTCH.

Come on, now … Let's meet Rosebud! *(Lights up on a table.)*

MATT. Uhhh, my name's Matt.

DEAN. I call all the gents "Butch" and all the gals "Rosebud." House rules. *(Barbie enters. She is completely "countrified," a woman hoping for a two-steppin' evening. A steel-girded Southern belle, she goes through men with a blowtorch. To Matt.)* There she is. Ain't she a beauty? Hey there, Rosebud. How you doin'?

BARBIE. Fine …

DEAN.

    WELL, LOOKEE WHAT JUST WALKED THROUGH MY DOOR!

    IS THIS WHAT YOU'VE BEEN WAITIN' FOR?

    BUTCH, THIS HERE IS ROSEBUD. WE'RE ALL GLAD YOU CAME.

BARBIE. Hi.

MATT. Hello. *(Handing her the flowers.)*

DEAN.

> ALRIGHT, SETTLE DOWN NOW. YOU KIDS STAY HERE.
>
> I'M GONNA RUSTLE US UP A PITCHER OF BEER.
>
> YOU TRY HARD NOT TO MISS ME. I'M GONNA DO THE SAME.

Whoa … Forgot the menus. *(Handing them menus shaped like pistols.)*

> BY THE BY, TRY THE NUMBER FOUR.
>
> IF YOU CAN CLEAN YOUR PLATE, WE'RE GONNA BRING YOU
>   MORE.
>
> IT COMES WITH ALL THE CORNBREAD YOU CAN CHEW.

And that's homemade …

> I'M GONNA GIVE Y'ALL A MINUTE JUST TO MAKE UP YOUR
>   MIND.
>
> GO AHEAD AND HOLLER IF THERE'S SOMETHING YOU CAN'T
>   FIND.
>
> AND HERE'S SOME HOT SAUCE MADE BY "YOU-KNOW-WHO."

Gotta big ole tub out back.

> AT DEAN'S OLD-FASHIONED ALL-AMERICAN
> DOWN-HOME BAR-B-QUE TEXAS EATS
> WHERE THE BEER'S ICE COLD AND THE CHILI'S RED HOT
> AND THE JUKEBOX CAN'T BE BEAT!
> WE GOT A BRISKET BASKET, LOADED SPUDS,
> WE GOT PEPPERS BATTER-FRIED.
> HELL! Y'ALL LOOK LIKE A COUPLE OF HAMMERED SHEEP.
> COME ON, LET OL' DEAN DECIDE FOR YA …

(Dean sizes up Barbie from head to foot, then decides on what she'll be ordering.)
Let's see now, Rosebud … you're gonna have a half-rack of Number Two. And
Butch *(Dean sizes Matt up in the same way.)* … Butch, I'll be damned if you ain't
gonna have a Chicken Caesar with the Caesar on the side, ain't ya?

MATT. And some green tea. *(Dean reacts as a true Texan would to such a request.
And then …)*

DEAN. Rosebud?

BARBIE. I'll have a Lone Star, no glass, wedge of lime.

DEAN. Rosebud, marry me now. *(A crash upstage in the kitchen.)* Trouble in the
kitchen. I'm gonna be right back atcha. *(He exits. Music begins.)*

BARBIE. *(From behind her flowers, smelling them.)* You're lookin' mighty fine in
that pocket protector over there.

MATT. Yeah?

BARBIE. Oh yeah. And I'm kinda curious 'bout what you're hidin' underneath
all that protection.

'CUZ IF I READ YOU RIGHT
YOU'RE A LITTLE UPTIGHT.
BUT THE RIGHT KINDA NIGHT
COULD CHANGE THAT.
I'LL BET YOU'RE WORTH THE CLIMB.
I'LL BET YOU TURN ON A DIME.
I'LL BET YOU TAKE YOUR TIME.
AND I'M JUST SAYIN'
YOU AND ME, BABE, WE COULD HAVE SOME FUN.
OR AM I JUMPIN' THE GUN?

(Dean enters with their drink orders. He sees that they are starting to come together, and quickly approaches the table.)

MATT. No, you're not jumpin' the gun at all!

BARBIE. Good.

DEAN. *(Quickly delivering their drinks.)* One Lone Star. One green tea. *(To Matt as he exits.)* Go get 'er, Butch.

MATT.

IT'S BEEN A WHILE, YOU KNOW.
I'M USED TO TAKIN' IT SLOW.
BUT I CAN "ROMEO"
WHEN I WANT TO.
AND I'D BE WILLIN' TO BET
THAT YOU CAN "JULIET."
AND THE NIGHT'S YOUNG YET.
AND PARTING WOULD BE SUCH SWEET SORROW FOR EVERY-
    ONE
OR AM I JUMPIN' THE GUN?

BARBIE. Hell, you're not jumpin' anything yet, sunshine. *(And she stands, and he follows suit. And soon they're dancing.)*

WE'LL TAKE A HANDFUL OF ME AND A HANDFUL OF YOU,
AND WE'LL MIX IT ALL TOGETHER AND WE'LL SEE WHAT IT
    CAN DO.
YEAH YEAH

MATT and BARBIE.

YEAH YEAH
WE GOTTA MINIMUM OF "NO" AND A WHOLE LOTTA "YES"
AND WHERE THE NIGHT'LL END UP IS ANYBODY'S GUESS!

BARBIE. This might not wait till the entrée.

MATT. I … I beg your pardon?

BARBIE.   I'm just sayin' … (*Giving him the hint.*) this … might … not …
WAIT … till the entrée.
MATT.

    I MAY BE WAY OFF-BASE,
    BUT WE COULD CUT TO THE CHASE.
    AND WE COULD HEAD TO MY PLACE
    FOR A NIGHTCAP.
BARBIE.

    WE COULD DITCH THESE RIBS
    AND THE PLASTIC BIBS,
    AND I'VE GOT DIBS ON EV'RY SQUARE INCH OF YOU, BABY.
    I'M GONNA START AT SQUARE ONE …
    OR AM I JUMPIN' THE GUN?
(*Pointing at different parts of Matt.*) And square two and three and four and …
BARBIE and MATT.

    WE'LL TAKE A HANDFUL OF ME AND A HANDFUL OF YOU
    AND WE'LL MIX IT ALL TOGETHER AND WE'LL SEE WHAT IT
      CAN DO.
    YEAH YEAH
    YEAH YEAH
    WE GOTTA MINIMUM OF "NO" AND A WHOLE LOTTA "YES"
    AND WHERE THE NIGHT'LL END UP IS ANYBODY'S GUESS!
    EH-ESS!
BARBIE.   (*As Matt recuperates.*) I swear, you better pace yourself. 'Cuz you're
gonna need every bit of energy you can muster. (*Matt reaches across the table and
finishes off her Lone Star in one gulp as she continues.*) Mmmmmmmmmm …

    SO IF WE'VE HAD OUR SAY
    I THINK IT'S TIME TO PLAY.
    'CUZ WE BEEN BURNIN' DAYLIGHT, BABY
MATT.

    THERE'S A WHOLE LOT MORE
    WE CAN BOTH EXPLORE
    WHEN WE CLOSE THE DOOR
BARBIE and MATT.

    AND IT'S YOU AND IT'S ME
    AND IT'S LOCK AND KEY.
    WE WON'T DISTURB NO ONE,
BARBIE.

    OR AM I JUMPIN' THE GUN?

BARBIE and MATT.
    I CAN GUARANTEE BEFORE THE NIGHT IS DONE,
    YOU AND I ARE JUMPIN' THE GUN.
(Dean enters as Matt and Barbie are hurriedly getting ready to leave.)
MATT. *(With a year's worth of urgency.)* Could we have the check, please?
DEAN. Comin' right up, Butch.
MATT. It's Matt. The name's Matt. *(A look of confusion from Barbie and the music begins with a bell tone. She pulls out a piece of paper from her cleavage. It's the email from her mistaken internet date.)*
BARBIE. Wait …
    SO YOUR NAME'S NOT KEN?
MATT. Nope, it's Matt.
BARBIE.
    HELL, IT'S HAPP'NING AGAIN.
MATT. What? What's happening?
BARBIE.
    THIS DATING SERVICE PROMISED ME MY …
    MY PRINCE AMONG MEN!
MATT. Well, what does my name matter?
BARBIE. Hon, my name is BARBIE. And I came here to FIND — MY — KEN!
    SO YOU'RE NOT FROM DAYTONA?
    YOU DON'T RACE CARS?
    YOU DON'T LIKE BEER JOINTS
    OR TWO-STEP BARS
    IS WHAT YOU'RE SAYIN' TO ME?
    HELL, I'M SUEING THIS DATING SERVICE THEN,
    'CUZ THEY PROMISED ME MY PRINCE WHOSE NAME WAS KEN.
MATT. I think you're taking this a little …
BARBIE.
    SO YOU DON'T COLLECT JOHN DEERE BASEBALL CAPS
    OR NAKED LADY TRUCK MUD FLAPS
    IS WHAT YOU'RE SAYIN' TO ME?
    THEY'VE BURNED MY HEART DOWN ONCE AGAIN,
    'CUZ I LOVED YOU WHEN I THOUGHT YOUR NAME WAS KEN.
    I'VE BEEN THROUGH A TWO O'CLOCK WITH MITCHELL,
    AND A FOUR O'CLOCK WITH STU.
    I'VE LIVED THROUGH SIX O'CLOCK WITH HENRY
    BEFORE MY EIGHT O'CLOCK WITH YOU.
    I'VE KISSED SO MANY FROGS SO MANY WAYS.

16

I WAS PUCKERED UP AGAIN.
BUT THE ONLY KISS YOU'LL GET'S "GOODBYE"
UNLESS YOUR NAME IS KEN!
AND YOU DON'T KNOW WHAT "FOLSOM PRISON" MEANS.
"MUSKOGEE" AIN'T NO HILL OF BEANS,
IS WHAT YOU'RE SAYIN' TO ME?
HELL, I WILL NOT SUFFER FOOLS AGAIN.
I'LL SAVE MY HEART FOR HIM WHOSE NAME IS KEN.

MATT. Barbie, can't we just talk about …

BARBIE.
SEE, YOU'RE NOT RAM TOUGH AND I HATE TO OFFEND,
BUT HEARTBREAK IS JUST UP AROUND THE BEND.
YOU WAIT AND SEE.
IT'S HAPPY TRAILS TO YOU, MY FRIEND.
'CUZ I LOVED YOU WHEN I THOUGHT YOUR NAME WAS KEN.

(Taking a bill from out of her cleavage as she starts to exit.)
I'M GONNA TAKE MY HEART BUT LEAVE A TEN.
'CUZ I LOVED YOU WHEN I THOUGHT YOUR NAME WAS …

(Dean enters in a hurry. Music stops.)

DEAN. Been a little mix-up here, kids. Rosebud, *(Pointing offstage.)* your date's at Table 2. *(Barbie sees the man of her dreams at the imagined offstage table, and sings the final note of the song.)*

BARBIE. KENNNNNN!!!

MATT. Then what table's MY date at?

DEAN. Butch, I guess your filly picked a table at a different stable. She's a NO-SHOW, Butch. *(Music.)* But don't you let this change your mind about love none. You get back up in that saddle, Butch, and brush off the dust. It's gonna be OK.
IF THE NIGHT HAS LEFT YOU LONELY WITH ITS PASSING,

MATT. It's only 8:15 …

DEAN.
AND IF THE DARKNESS FALLS ALL AROUND YOU AND HIDES
YOUR WAY.
DEEP IN THE BREAKING OF YOUR HEART
THERE'S A LIGHT THAT'S TRYING TO START.
YOU JUST KEEP REACHING FOR THE BREAKING OF THE DAY.
Come on, Butch. Buck up.
BECAUSE A NEW DAY SHINES A NEW LIGHT ON NEW HORIZONS.
AND THE ROAD BECOMES MUCH CLEARER WITH THE DAWN.
PACK UP YOUR TROUBLES GOOD AND TIGHT

AND KISS YOUR WORRYING HEART "GOOD NIGHT,"
AND WITH THE MORNING LIGHT TAKE YOUR CUE TO CARRY
ON.

Alright, Butch … your turn.

MATT.
MORNING LIGHT UPON ME …

DEAN.
CHANGES NIGHT TO BRIGHTEST DAY.

MATT.
AND-UH MORNING LIGHT SHINE ON ME,

DEAN.
TAKE MY HAND AND GUIDE MY WAY.

MATT.
THROUGH THE DARKNESS OF THIS VALLEY

DEAN.
FILL MY HEART AND LIFT MY EYES.

Sing it with me.

DEAN and MATT
I-I AM EMPTY WITH THIS TRAVELLIN' BUT I'M A-REACHIN' FOR
THE PRIZE.

MATT.
WHEN THE NIGHT HAS LEFT ME LONELY WITH ITS PASSING

DEAN. That's it, Butch. You get it ALL out.

MATT.
AND WHEN THE DARKNESS FALLS ALL AROUND ME AND HIDES
MY WAY.

DEAN. Butch, you sing us all proud.

DEAN and MATT.
DEEP IN THE BREAKING OF YOUR HEART,
THERE'S A LIGHT THAT'S TRYIN' TO START.
YOU JUST KEEP REACHIN' FOR THE BREAKING OF THE DAY

DEAN. That's it, Butch. Keep on reachin'.

DEAN and MATT.
MORNING LIGHT UPON ME CHANGES NIGHT TO BRIGHTEST
DAY.
AND-UH MORNING LIGHT SHINE ON ME, TAKE MY HAND AND
GUIDE MY WAY.
THROUGH THE DARKNESS OF THIS VALLEY FILL MY HEART
AND LIFT MY EYES.

MATT.
> I'M EMPTY WITH THIS TRAVELLIN' BUT I'M REACHIN' FOR THE PRIZE.

DEAN. You drive safe now, Butch … *(He exits.)*

MATT.
> I'M EMPTY WITH THIS TRAVELLIN' BUT I'M REACHIN' FOR THE PRIZE.
> I'M SO EMPTY WITH THIS TRAVELLIN' … *(Band out.)*
> WHEN WILL I SEE LOVE
> LOOKING BACK AT ME? *(Band in.)*
> I'VE BEEN WAITING HERE PATIENTLY
> CAN YOU PLEASE FIND YOUR WAY?
> SOMEONE UP ABOVE
> REACH DOWN GENTLY AND GUIDE MY LOVE
> I'VE BEEN HOPING SO LONG
> THAT LOVE WOULD LOOK BACK
> AT ME.

(Blackout as Matt exits, and Sofia enters, making out with Gino, and on her cell phone, mid-phone call to her husband, Nicky, a mob boss.)

SOFIA.
> NICKY, DON'T SHOUT!
> IT'S JUST "LADIES NIGHT OUT," NICKY!
> DINNER AND SOME GIRL TALK.
> I'LL BE HOME BEFORE LETTERMAN'S THROUGH!
> NICKY, NO MORE!
> WE'VE BEEN THROUGH THIS BEFORE, NICKY!
> PUT IT IN THE MICROWAVE!
> NUKE IT THREE MINUTES, YOU'RE THROUGH, NICKY …
> NOT SUCH A TOUGH THING TO DO, NICKY …
> JUST A COUPLE HOURS

(Smooch to Gino who then exits.)
> ME TOO, NICKY.

(She hangs up the phone, then talks to it.) Damn you, Nicky Pizzicato!
> THOSE EYES, THAT WOULD SEE INTO MY EYES SO CLEARLY.
> THOSE ARMS, THAT WOULD HOLD ME AND NOT LET ME LEAVE.
> THOSE LIPS, THAT WOULD KISS AWAY ALL OF OUR EVENINGS.
> AND THAT!!! I'VE NOT FONDLED SINCE LAST NEW YEAR'S EVE!
> OH MY GOD, IF NICKY KNEW
> ALL OF THE SNEAKY LITTLE TRICKS WE DO!

THE MARINARA I THOUGHT WE HAD,
OR THE CHEESE WENT BAD.
I'LL JUST GET SOME MORE
AND I RUN TO THE STORE,
BUT NOT REALLY …
I SAY I DO, BUT NOT REALLY.
OH MY GOD, IF NICKY KNEW
THAT SOMEONE DOES ME LIKE HE USED TO DO.
THE KIND OF HELL GINO'D HAVE TO PAY
IN A PAINFUL WAY.
BEATEN BLACK AND BLUE
THAT'S THE LEAST HE WOULD DO,
IF MY NICKY KNEW.
IF NICKY KNEW!

(Carlo enters, the head waiter here. Carlo is an informant for Nicky, and lives in perpetual fear that Nicky will discover the affair between Sofia and Gino. He is never not moving in some way; a moving target is safer than one who stands still. He weaves through a sea of invisible tables as he sings out to us.)
CARLO. *Scuzi, scuzi, scuzi, SCUZI …*

SOFIA AND GINO, THEY HAVE THE AFFAIR.
Scuzi, SCUZI …

THEY COME AT ODD HOURS. THEY SIT OVER THERE.
THEY KISS AND THEY CUDDLE BEHIND NICKY'S BACK.
AND EVERY TIME I GET A PANIC ATTACK.
'CUZ IF I MAKE A FUSS, THEN THEY GIVE ME THE SACK.
BUT IF NICKY SEES GINO THEN SOMEONE GETS WHACKED!
Ohhhhhhh, I gotta bad, bad feeling about this … Something's-a gonna happen.
AND IF SOMEONE GETS WHACKED, THEN WHO WILL IT BE?
Scuzi, scuzi …

WILL NICKY WHACK GINO OR WILL HE WHACK ME?
'CUZ GINO IS GETTING TOO BIG FOR HIS BRITCHES,
AND NICKY IS STARTING TO WONDER "WHAT GIVES?" WHICH IS
USUALLY WHERE I END UP WITH THE STITCHES …
I'M NICKY'S EYES. I KNOW THE DIRT.
I SAY WHAT I SEE. THAT WAY I DON'T GET HURT!
Oh my God, Nicky's gonna kill me! Gino, you SON OF A BITCH! *(Gino enters. He and Sofia have been making out in the kitchen. She joins Gino at the table, rearranging herself as she enters. Gino has a huge chip on his shoulder, being a mere lieutenant in the "family," and forever wondering why Nicky is in charge.)*

20

GINO. He better watch his back, Sofia. That's all I'm sayin'. He better watch his frickin' back.

> IT'S ALWAYS NICKY. I'M SICK OF NICKY.
> EVERYWHERE NICKY THIS AND NICKY THAT.
> I'M THROUGH
> IT'S GONNA BE SO SWEET
> WHEN GINO BREAKS HIM IN TWO.
> NICKY, WATCH WHAT YOU DO,
> 'CUZ GINO'S COMING FOR YOU.

All these years, Nicky. I've been waiting all these frickin' years …

> IT'S TIME FOR GINO. REMEMBER GINO?
> THE ONE WHO'S GOT YOUR BACK?
> WHO TAKES YOUR FLACK?
> WELL, THAT'S THROUGH.
> FROM NOW ON GINO DOES WHAT GINO WANTS TO DO.
> AND GINO WANTS A FAMILY COUP.
> NICKY, I'M COMING FOR YOU!

(Very stylized movement as they become one mass of operatic humanity.)

SOFIA.	CARLO.	GINO.
		OH MY GOD, IF NICKY KNEW
OH GINO!	HE'S GONNA KILL ME! BULLETS WILL DRILL ME!	THAT GINO'S COMING WITH A WRECKING CREW.
NO, GINO!	I MAYBE GET A RUN-NING START.	AND NICKY ALL OF YOUR DAYS ARE DONE
ON MY KNEES.	I FEEL THEM SHOOT-ING THROUGH MY HEART.	BEING NUMBER ONE. WHEN I'M THROUGH WITH YOU, YOU'LL BE NUMBER TWO.
GINO PLEASE!	I'M TRYING NOT TO FALL APART BUT FIRST I'M RUN-NING FOR THE DOOR.	THAT'S YOU, NICKY.
GINO, GO SLOW.	AND THEN I'M LYING ON THE FLOOR.	NUMBER TWO NOW, NICKY.
NO, GINO, NO!	AND I'M NOT BREATH-ING ANYMORE!	

21

SOFIA.	CARLO.	GINO.
OH MY GOD,	OH MY GOD,	OH MY GOD,
IF NICKY KNEW	IF NICKY KNEW	IF NICKY KNEW
THE KIND OF MISERY	THE KIND OF MISERY	THE KIND OF MISERY
HE DROVE ME TO!	HE DROVE ME TO!	HE DROVE ME TO!
NIGHT AFTER NIGHT		
I CRY COUNTLESS		
TEARS!		
		WAITING ALL THESE
		YEARS!
	AND I GUARANTEE	
	HE WILL MURDER ME	
IF HE DISCOVERS	IF HE DISCOVERS	IF HE DISCOVERS
TWO SECRET LOVERS!	TWO SECRET LOVERS!	TWO SECRET LOVERS!
	THERE'S A-GONNA BE	
	HELL TO PAY!!!	
IF NICKY KNEW!	IF NICKY KNEW!	IF NICKY KNEW!

CARLO. *Scuzi, scuzi, scuzi, SCUZI!!!*

(A crash from the kitchen upstage.)

CARLO. Trouble in the kitchen. *(He exits.)*

GINO. Sofia, what gives? You're not yourself tonight.

SOFIA.

> I'VE COME HERE TO TELL YOU THAT THIS HAS TO END, GINO!
> TONIGHT WHEN WE LEAVE HERE, WE LEAVE HERE AS
> FRIENDS, GINO!
> NOTHING MORE
> I IMPLORE YOU,
> IT'S SHEER HEARTACHE!
> I'M WORTH MORE GINO,
> SO MUCH MORE!

GINO.

> SOFIA, DON'T TELL ME OUR LOVE IS THROUGH!
> YOU SHATTER MY HEART IF YOU TEAR US IN TWO, SOFIA,
> NOTHING LESS.
> YOUR CARESS IS LIKE BREATH TO ME!
> NOTHING LESS, SOFIA!
> NOTHING LESS!

SOFIA. I'm telling you, Gino, nothing good can come from this.

GINO. Sofia …

GIVE ME THIS NIGHT,
I ASK FOR ONE NIGHT ONLY.
JUST ONE MORE NIGHT ALONE
THEN LEAVE ME LONELY.
COME WHAT MAY,
GIVE ME ONE MORE DAY,
FOR WHEN OUR DAYS TOGETHER
ARE GONE FOREVER.

SOFIA.
GIVE ME THIS NIGHT
WITHOUT THE FEAR I CLING TO.
GIVE ME ONE NIGHT
WHERE UNASHAMED I BRING YOU ALL MY HEART
NOT THIS TINY PART.
BUT MY HEART'S BESPOKEN.

GINO.
AND NOW MINE'S BROKEN.

GINO and SOFIA.
YOU,
ME AND YOU,
SOMETHING GREW.
SOMETHING BEAUTIFUL.
BUT TIME
STOPPED ITS CLIMB.
STOLE ITS PRIME.
WHAT WAS BEAUTIFUL IS GONE.
NOW WE MOVE ON.

(Gino instinctively goes to Sofia. He takes her by the hand and then starts to embrace her. She backs away from him.)

GINO. Sofia …

SOFIA. No, Gino …

GINO.

GIVE ME THIS NIGHT,
THOUGH I MAY GET NO OTHERS.
ONE FINAL NIGHT
FOR ME AND YOU AS LOVERS
LIVE TONIGHT.
JUST HOLD ME TIGHT,
THEN LET GO TOMORROW …

SOFIA.

HOW CAN I GIVE WHAT I DON'T
HAVE TO GIVE, GINO?
I WILL NOT HELP THIS LOVE TO
LIVE TONIGHT.
JUST HOLD ME TIGHT.

SOFIA.

    NO, GINO, WE LET GO NOW.

GINO.

    AND DRINK UP SORROW …

SOFIA.

    OH, GINO …

(Sofia and Gino embrace. Carlo enters holding a phone receiver and pulling a phone cord through the double kitchen doors.)

CARLO. *Scuzi, scuzi, SCUZI, SCUZI!!!* Mrs. a-Pizzicato, it's Nicky! And he KNOWS!!! *(Music starts.)* I never told him, Mrs. a-Pizzicato. I swear to you I NEVER …

SOFIA. *(Overlapping him, but with the music.)* Shhhhh! Give me the phone. *(Gino and Carlo lean into Sofia to hear the phone conversation. Sofia clears her throat.)*

    NICKY, I SAID I'D BE HOME IN A FEW.

CARLO.

    OH MY GOD …

SOFIA. Shhhh!!!

    BUT I'M KINDA TIRED, SO MAYBE I'M THROUGH

(Into the phone.) Yeah, we're winding down.

    SO NICKY STAY PUT HONEY, RIGHT WHERE YOU ARE.

    I'LL FINISH MY DRINK WITH THE GIRLS AT THE BAR.

    THEN I'M HEADED FOR HOME, AND IT ISN'T THAT FAR.

    NICKY, WHAT DO YOU MEAN THAT YOU'RE OUT IN THE CAR?!

(Car headlights immediately illuminate the three huddled on the phone.) Oh, shit! He's out in the parking lot!

CARLO. What are we gonna do? WHAT ARE WE GONNA DO?

GINO. Give me the frickin' phone, Sophia! *(Carlo gets tied in a Gordian knot with the phone cord while Sofia and Gino sing at Nicky, both into the phone and out into the audience/parking lot.)*

SOFIA.	GINO.
NICKY, YOU'RE MAKING THIS INTO A STINK!	
	HOW'S IT FEEL, NICKY?!
YOU'RE OVERREACTING.	
I KNOW HOW YOU THINK!	
	LOUSY DEAL, NICKY!!!

SOFIA.

    BUT NOTHING YOU'VE SEEN IS WORTH FUSSING ABOUT.

    I'LL COME TO THE CAR AND WE'LL WORK IT ALL OUT.

    YOU AND ME, NICKY, WE'LL SOLVE IT ALONE.

GINO.
    OH FOR CRYING OUT LOUD, WILL YA GIVE ME THE PHONE?!
(Gino grabs the phone from Sofia and pushes her aside, perhaps into Carlo.)

GINO.	SOFIA.	CARLO.
NOW NICKY KNOWS!		GINO!
	GINO, WHAT ARE	GINO!
	YOU DOING?	GINO!
GINO'S WAITING IS		
THROUGH!		NICKY!
	NICKY, DON'T LISTEN!	NICKY!
		NICKY!
YOU TAKE SOME-		
THING FROM ME!		
	OH MY GOD, GINO,	OH MY GOD, GINO,
	WHY, GINO?	WHY, GINO?
I TAKE SOMETHING		HE'LL TAKE EVERY-
FROM YOU!		THING
	HE'LL TAKE EVERY-	
	THING.	GINO …

GINO.
    I WAS NEXT IN LINE, NICKY.
    THE FAM'LY WAS MINE, NICKY!
    YOU WALTZ INTO THE PICTURE
    AND YOU TAKE AWAY ALL OF MY DREAMS!

SOFIA. *(She tries to take the phone from Gino.)* Gino, what are you saying?!

GINO. Shut up, Sofia. *(Pushing her aside.)*
    SO HOW DOES IT FEEL, NICKY?
    DOES IT CUT LIKE COLD STEEL, NICKY?
    NOW WE'VE SHARED SOFIA,
    YOU AND ME SHARE ONE MORE THING … THE PAIN, NICKY.
    DO YOU FEEL THAT ICE IN YOUR VEINS, NICKY?
    A WARMTH YOU'LL NEVER REGAIN, NICKY.
    YOU AND ME GOT SOME BUS'NESS NOW, NICKY.
    I'M COMING OUT THERE AND WE'LL SEE IF MISTER MOB BOSS
    IN ALL OF HIS INFINITE WISDOM
    KNOWS HOW TO MAKE THIS THING RIGHT.

I'll be right out, Nicky. Put your piece on the dash. *(Headlights go out. He hands Carlo the phone.)* Beat it, Carlo. *(Carlo exits, nervously, raveled up in the cord. Gino gets ready to leave.)*

25

SOFIA. Are you telling me, Gino, that this whole thing has been a lie?
GINO.

    I AIMED FOR NICKY
    AND ONLY NICKY.
    YOU WERE THE QUICKEST WAY
    TO LURE THE PREY.
    DON'T YOU SEE?
    THANKS FOR THE HELPING HAND,
    WENT OFF JUST LIKE I PLANNED.
    YOU WERE THE KEY.

Wake up, Sofia!
    THERE IS NO "YOU AND ME,"
    AND THERE NEVER WILL BE.

(Sofia crosses into Gino. She nestles into him, still singing out, he wraps his arms around her.)
SOFIA.

    BUT TELL ME, GINO ...
    HOW COULD YOU, GINO?
    DON'T YOU FEEL ANYTHING AT ALL FOR ME, GINO?

GINO.	SOFIA.
MY POOR SOFIA,	NO, GINO.
NO MORE SOFIA.	PLEASE, GINO.
YOU PAYED A HEFTY PRICE,	IT'S
YOU LOST YOUR LOVER TWICE.	MUCH TOO HIGH A
TRAGIC, BUT TRUE.	PRICE TO PAY.
	FIRST HIM, NOW
	YOU. NO, GINO.
MAYBE HE'LL TAKE YOU BACK	I DON'T WANT HIM.
ALTHOUGH HIS HEART IS CRACKED,	THERE'S ONLY YOU, GINO.
BROKEN IN TWO	WE'VE CLIMBED TO NOW
WILL YOU START OVER NEW?	FROM NEVER.
OR WILL NICKY TELL YOU YOU'RE ...	OUR LOVE WILL LAST FOREVER ...

(A gunshot is heard. Gino steps away from Sofia, and we see that she is holding a pistol on him.)
SOFIA. Damn you, Gino ... *(Gino gasps for air, dying tragically and rhythmically to the music. She puts the gun away, pulls out her cell phone, dials a number, and faces straight out to Nicky in the parking lot.)*
    GINO IS THROUGH, NICKY.
    WHAT MORE CAN I DO, NICKY?

YES. I'M COMING TO THE CAR NOW.
AT LEAST HEAR ME OUT, NICKY
PLEASE …

(Headlights flash an "OK." She turns to Gino, dead on the floor.) Goodbye, Gino … *(Sofia steps down to us, pulls out a compact, readjusts her face, as the music swells underneath her. She exits the Trattoria as thunder strikes and lightning flashes. Gino's body is dragged offstage. Heimlich enters. He is the head waiter at a German restaurant, Der Schlupfwinkel Speiseplatz. It is a dark and stormy night. He talks out to the audience as if it were a couple just ducking in from the rain.)*

HEIMLICH.   *Guten abend, meine freunden.* Come in, come in. You'll be drenched. On such a night no soul should be out in the streets, we should all find someplace warm und dry. Welcome to Der Schlupfwinkel Speiseplatz. A little refuge in a big city. Here, let me take your coats; the storm looks like it will be here for a while.

CLOUDS MOVING FAST.
RAIN FALLING HARDER.
POURING DOWN IN SHEETS NOW.
PELTING AGAINST THE PANE.
STORM'S BOUND TO LAST.
GROWING DARKER UND DARKER.
UND EACH OF US NEEDS SHELTER,
SOME REFUGE FROM THE RAIN.

Some come to the Schlupfwinkel for the menu. Others come here for quite a different reason altogether. *(Lights up on an empty spot onstage where Heimlich imagines a girl sitting alone at a "table.")* Here's such a one by the window …

A SIMPLE GIRL AT THE START,
HER LOVER SIMPLY ADORED HER,
UND LIKE SO MANY SIMPLE THINGS,
HE SIMPLY STOPPED ONE DAY.
SHE NEVER HAD A BROKEN HEART,
TILL THE MAN BROKE IT FOR HER
UND NOW SHE'S HERE FOR SHELTER
WHERE SHE TUCKS HER LOVE AWAY.

(Lights down on that "table.") Always sits by that window und looks. Und none of us knows what for. *(Lights up on another "table.")* Und over here's another one …

HE WORKED HARD ALL HIS DAYS
UND HE ROSE UP THE LADDER
UND HE HAD NO TIME FOR ANYTHING
AS HE CLIMBED WAY UP HIGH.

THEN THE MACHINE TOOK HIS PLACE
UND HIS PRESENCE DIDN'T MATTER.
UND HE'S FALLEN HERE FOR SHELTER
WHERE HE WATCHES HIS TIME GO BY.

There are so many different things to hide from, aren't there? The rain ... the time ... your heart ...

SO HERE'S YOUR HIDING PLACE ...
STAY A WHILE OR MAYBE LONGER.
BUT WHILE YOU LICK YOUR WOUNDS, REMEMBER
THAT LIFE MARCHES ON.
UND WHEN YOU JUMP BACK IN THE RACE
LET'S HOPE YOUR HEART'S A LITTLE STRONGER,
FOR THE ONLY POINT OF SHELTER
IS WHAT YOU'LL DO ONCE YOUR SHELTER'S GONE.

We will begin seating in just a minute. Please, make yourselves comfortable. I should introduce myself to you. My name is Heimlich *(The band coughs.)*, und I'm the head waiter here at the Speiseplatz. *(A crash from the kitchen upstage.)* Trouble in the kitchen. *(He starts to exit, but sees a woman in the wings, entering the restaurant. Music chord.)* No! It's impossible! What is SHE doing here? She said she was visiting her sick auntie in Hamburg for the whole week. *(Music out.)* Ladies und gentlemen, my secret girlfriend whom I told never to meet me here ever under any circumstances whatsoever: Gretchen! *(Gretchen enters. She is dressed in a dominatrix outfit. Leather, riding crop, boots, military perhaps. Heimlich hides. She takes the stage and surveys the audience, before settling into the song.)*

GRETCHEN.

THEY TELL ME THAT THE ESKIMOS
HAVE FIFTY WORDS FOR "SNOW,"
UND THE FRENCH USE MANY MORE
TO SPEAK OF "LOVE."
UND WHEN A GIRL REFUSES SEX
SHE NEEDS A HUNDRED WORDS FOR "NO"
SINCE MOST MEN FIND IT HARD

(Accusing a man in her view.) Don't you?

TO RISE ABOVE.
I'D SAY IT ONE WAY TO HIS FACE,
UND QUITE ANOTHER IN HIS EAR.
UND ON ONE OCCASION, SEMAPHORE,
AS THE SHIP WAS LEAVING PIER

It was to an entire deckful of sailors I had met on shore leave the night before.

They were each sweet in their own way, but collectively, it was time-prohibitive to keep up all of their … hopes … at once. *(Music.)* I'm sure each of you has had a similar experience.

> IF I'M IMPRESSED,
> UND NOT TOO STRESSED
> THEN I MIGHT ANSWER, "YES,"
> BUT "NO" IS A WORD I DON'T FEAR!
> A BIT OF "JA"
> GOES PRETTY FAR
> IF HE'S GOT A NICE OOM PAH PAH
> BUT "NEIN"

Unless it's 9
Is it ever 9, girls?
No …

> NOWHERE NEAR!
> I'D RATHER SAY, "NO"
> RIGHT FROM THE GET-GO
> THAN TO LEAD SOMEONE BLITHELY ALONG.
> WHY TAKE ALL THE PAINS
> MIT THE WHIPS UND THE CHAINS
> IF YOU KNOW THAT THIS UNION
> IS HORRIBLY WRONG?

We have so little time, don't we? Girls, why waste it on little men?

> IF I SEE
> HE'S MY CUP OF TEA,
> THEN I MIGHT ANSWER, "OUI!"
> BUT "NON" IS A WORD I DON'T FEAR!
> IF HE'S PROUD
> THAT HE'S ENDOWED,
> I'LL SHOUT A "YES" RIGHT OUT LOUD,
> BUT PLEASE SIR,

If I need a tweezer …
Have you been there before, girls?
Believe me …

> STEER CLEAR!
> IF HE BROACHES THE TOPIC
> UND HE'S MICROSCOPIC
> I'LL NOT HEAR ONE WORD OF HIS CASE.
> BUT WHEN THIGHS CATCH MY EYES

UND THEN GENEROUS SIZE,
I'M STUCK BETWEEN A ROCK
UND A VERY HARD PLACE!

I'm telling you because I know, girls! *(Gretchen mumbles some lines as she kicks the chairs across the stage ... something like ... "Why doesn't anyone listen to me? I've been telling them for years now!!!")*

TO CONCLUDE
WITHOUT BEING RUDE
UNLESS I SENSE MAGNITUDE,
I'M SURE THAT YOU KNOW WHAT YOU'LL HEAR.
FOR A "YES"
HE MUST BE BLESSED
MIT A CERTAIN LARGESSE,
FOR "NO," "NO" IS A WORD I DON'T FEAR!

I'm just up the street a bit. Make sure you bring a measuring stick! *(Song ends. She crosses to Heimlich who has emerged from the wings.)*

HEIMLICH. Gretchen, what on earth are you doing here?

GRETCHEN. There you are, Heimlich. *(She and the band cough.)* I thought you had a shift here tonight.

HEIMLICH. Gretchen, I asked you never to meet me here ever under any circumstances whatsoever.

GRETCHEN. I know, Heimlich. *(She and the band cough.)*, und normally I would obey such a request. But this is urgent. I've come to tell you ... that we are now over.

HEIMLICH. Over?

GRETCHEN. Kaput, Heimlich. *(She and the band cough.)* I know I told you I was visiting my sick auntie in Hamburg this whole week, but really I have been barricaded in my flat mit a new lover. You'd like him. Which reminds me ... *(Pulling out a pair of frilly girlie panties.)* I've also come to return these frilly girlie panties you left behind after our last encounter. I can bear the sight of them no longer. *Auf Wiedersehen*, Heimlich. *(She and the band cough.)* Klaus will be wondering where I've gone to ...

KLAUS. *(Offstage.)* Gretchen dearest?

HEIMLICH. *(Pedal tone music.)* No! It's impossible! What is HE doing here? He told me he would be away on company business in Stuttgart this whole week. *(Music out. Klaus enters hurriedly. He looks as if he has been dipped in glue and shot through a sex toy store, grabbing one of every item along the way. He is clearly Gretchen's new plaything. He crosses right in front of Heimlich and speaks to Gretchen.)*

KLAUS. There you are ... *(Seeing how Gretchen is dressed in public.)* Gretchen!!!

HEIMLICH. Klaus!!!

KLAUS. *(Seeing Heimlich.)* Heimlich!!! *(Everyone but Heimlich coughs.)* I had no idea you were working tonight. *(Out to audience.)* How suddenly uncomfortable … *(Pedal tone music.)*

HEIMLICH. Ladies und gentlemen, my secret BOYfriend whom I ALSO told never to meet me here ever under any circumstances whatsoever … *(Music out.)* … Klaus. *(Song begins.)*

KLAUS. Gretchen, have you been here all this while mit this man? What can this mean?

> YOU SAID YOU WOULD BE BACK REAL SOON,
> BUT SOON YOU WERE NOT BACK.
> SO I UNDID ALL THE CHAINS
> UND I CLIMBED DOWN FROM OFF THE RACK.
> UND I THREW ON WHAT I COULD
> UND FOUND YOU QUICKLY AS COULD BE,
> 'CUZ YOU PROMISED YOU WOULD DO
> DER BUMSEN-KRATZENTANZ MIT ME!

KLAUS, GRETCHEN and HEIMLICH.

> YOU PROMISED YOU WOULD DO
> DER BUMSEN-KRATZENTANZ MIT ME!

HEIMLICH. Did you promise to do such a dance mit this man?

GRETCHEN. I may have said something to that effect.

KLAUS. Ja, you did! Und you said if I was very good, you would teach me this dance. Und I have been very good all week, ja?

GRETCHEN. Ja …

> YOU USED EACH LITTLE TOY, MEIN GOTT!
> UND EV'RY COSTUME FITS!
> YOU LASTED ALL THIS WEEK
> WHERE OTHER MEN WOULD CALL IT QUITS!
> YOU CONTINUE TO SURPRISE ME
> MIT EACH WHOPPING THING YOU DO,
> BUT I STILL DON'T KNOW IF I WILL
> BUMSEN-KRATZENTANZ MIT YOU!

KLAUS, GRETCHEN and HEIMLICH.

> I STILL DON'T KNOW IF I WILL
> BUMSEN-KRATZENTANZ MIT YOU!

HEIMLICH. Is there no bottom to my despair? *(Klaus raises his hand.)* While it is heartbreaking for either one of you to appear here in this way to me, it is out of all thinking that two such disparate parts of my life should be so conjoined.

> I WAS DATING BOTH OF YOU,

OR HAS THIS SLIPPED YOUR MINDS?
NOW YOU TWO ARE MOVING ON TOGETHER
LEAVING ME BEHIND!
UND THE CROWNING DEGRADATION,
FROM WHICH I CANNOT FLEE,
IS THAT NEITHER OF YOU CARED TO
BUMSEN-KRATZENTANZ MIT ME!

KLAUS, GRETCHEN and HEIMLICH.
NEITHER OF YOU CARED TO
BUMSEN-KRATZENTANZ MIT ME!

GRETCHEN. It is a powerful dance. It knows no genders, no boundaries whatsoever. We will do this dance for you now, as both a "hello" und a "goodbye" to this moment. (*They dance the Bumsen-Kratzentanz. Note to choreographer: "bumsen" equals sex, and "kratzentanz" is a word I made up meaning "scratching dance." This dance should be a continuous coupling of different sexual positions between the three of them, and we should be crying with laughter by the end of it.*) Klaus?

KLAUS. Yes, Gretchen.

GRETCHEN. When we are done, I want you to return to meine flat und re-attach yourself to the rack mit the chains.

KLAUS. Yes, Gretchen.

GRETCHEN. Heimlich, (*Everyone but Heimlich coughs.*) I want you to move on from this parting mit your head held high.

MY HEART IS TAKING WING
UND I FEEL LIGHTER THAN A FEATHER
FROM THE PASSION WE'VE IGNITED
WHEN THINGS RUB TOO CLOSE TOGETHER.
I COULD WISH NO GREATER HAPPINESS
TO LAST YOUR LIFETIME THROUGH
THAN THAT SOMEDAY SOMEONE ELSE WILL
BUMSEN-KRATZENTANZ MIT YOU!

KLAUS, GRETCHEN and HEIMLICH.
THAT SOMEDAY SOMEONE ELSE WILL
BUMSEN — KRATZ — EN — TANZ MIT YOU!
HEY!

(*They separate from whatever "connected" positions they have encountered while performing the dance. A light of recognition happens between Klaus and Heimlich. Music begins, and then ... *)

KLAUS. Gretchen?

GRETCHEN. Yes, Klaus?

HEIMLICH and KLAUS.
    THE TWO OF US HAVE SOME REGRET
    THAT IN THE DANCE WE THREE HAVE JUST PERFORMED
    A CERTAIN FEELING HAS BEEN REKINDLED.
GRETCHEN. What are you saying, boys?
HEIMLICH and KLAUS.
    WE'RE SAYING LOVE IS NOT A CONSTANT GUEST,
    UND WHO CAN KNOW WHEN IT WILL COME OR GO?
    SO IF IT'S HERE, TAKE HANDS UND RISK LOVE.
(Klaus and Heimlich take hands, and then sing to Gretchen as they wave to her, exiting …)
HEIMLICH and KLAUS.
    RISK LOVE,
    RISK LOVE!
(Heimlich and Klaus exit together. Gretchen cleans her face of all her make-up, and lets her hair down, perhaps literally. Sits in a chair and sings out to us.)
GRETCHEN. Ah, the boys are gone. It is so very rare with me these days, that the boys are ever gone.
    YOU'D THINK MIT ALL THE ENDLESS MEN
    THAT I WOULD NEVER BE ALONE AGAIN
    IT'S COMMON KNOWLEDGE THAT I'M APTLY SKILL'D.
    WHY IS MY DANCE CARD NEVER LESS THAN FILL'D?
I'll tell you why …
    LUST CAN OFTEN LEAD TO MORE
    IF THAT MEANS LOVE, I TEND TO SHUT THE DOOR.
    SO MUCH BETTER I SHOULD LOCK MY HEART,
    THAN RISK REPEATING HOW IT BROKE APART.
    NOW MAN AFTER MAN,
    I AM BATTLING INSIDE.
    DO I REACH OUT FOR LOVE?
    DO I TREMBLE UND HIDE?
    I'M MUCH MORE CONTENT
    MIT A MAN WHO WILL SEE
    ONLY ONE INCH BENEATH
    ALL THE MILES THAT ARE ME.
    IT'S MUCH MORE SAFE TO PLAY MIT FIRE
    TO RUN YOUR FINGERS THROUGH A MAN'S DESIRE
    UND IF THE HEAT'S TOO HIGH A PRICE TO PAY
    THEN YOU CAN ALWAYS PULL YOUR HAND AWAY.

BUT LOVE WON'T LET YOU PULL APART
IF YOU'VE PROMISED SOMEONE ELSE YOUR HEART.
ONCE YOU'VE WRAPPED YOURSELVES UP GOOD UND TIGHT
YOU WON'T BREAK FREE AGAIN MIT-OUT A FIGHT.
UND I WAS BUT A GIRL
WHEN MY HEART LEARNED FOR GOOD,
LOVE WILL BREAK YOU MORE DEEPLY
THAN LUST EVER COULD.
NOW ALL THE KING'S HORSES
UND ALL THE KING'S MEN
CANNOT PUT THIS HEART …

(She cannot bring herself to say "back together again." She gathers her trappings and gets ready to exit, crossing upstage.)

LOVE PROVIDED SUCH A SCARE
NOW LUST IS REALLY ALL I DARE.
UND IF MY HEART WERE NOT SO BRUISED,
I WONDER WHICH I'M MORE INCLINED TO CHOOSE?

(As Gretchen exits, Guillermo enters, turning back to an "unseen victim." He threatens the offstage man at gunpoint.)

GUILLERMO. Choose now, *señor*. Your money or your life? Haaaa ha ha ha ha! *(An offstage hand presents a bag of money. Guillermo takes it and exits. Ernesto enters, singing the ballad of this renegade outlaw. As he does so, Guillermo enacts various gallant poses at the end of each line.)*

ERNESTO.

LISTEN TO THE TALE OF A RENEGADE MAN.
WHO BATTLES INJUSTICE WHENEVER HE CAN.
THOUGH THE PEOPLE ARE THANKFUL HE FIGHTS IN THEIR
    NAME,
THEY SECRETLY WISH HE'D GO BACK WHERE HE CAME.

GUILLERMO. *(Entering and speaking out to the control booth of the theatre.)* Hold! Hoooooolllld! HOOOOOOOOLLLLLLLLDDD!!! *(The pit stops playing.)* OK … *(To Ernesto.)* "They secretly wish he'd go back where he came?" That's not the lyric, OK? You gonna sing MY song, mister, you gonna sing it the way it was written. *(Out to the booth.)* Let's take it back from the end of the German girl with the bruised heart. *(He exits muttering some Mexican obscenities to himself. Gretchen reenters out of costume, mid-quick change. The pit starts to play. The business with Guillermo and the hold-up is enacted exactly as it was before.)*

GRETCHEN. *(Taking her exit again.)*

UND IF MY HEART WERE NOT SO BRUISED,

I WONDER WHICH I'M MORE INCLINED TO CHOOSE?

GUILLERMO. Choose now, *señor.* Your money or your life? Haaaa ha ha ha ha ha!

ERNESTO.

LISTEN TO THE TALE OF A BANDIT I KNOW
WHO FIGHTS FOR THE RIGHTS TO A FREE MEXICO.
BUT THE LAW CAN OUTSMART HIM AT EVERY PASS,
'CUZ HIS HEAD'S PLANTED FIRMLY THREE FEET UP HIS …

GUILLERMO. *(Entering from offstage.)* HOLLLLLLD!!! *(To Ernesto.)* Ok, look … I don't know if you got some "little man" stuff you wanna work out with somebody maybe sometime, but for now you singing "The Ballad of *Guillermo.*" So sing the damn song, mister, or we gonna have some trouble. *(Gretchen reenters, thinking we're going back to the same place. Guillermo speaks out to the booth.)* I don't need the German girl. *(Gretchen, who has not fully entered, exits.)* We take it right from where he sing. *(Music begins, and as Guillermo exits he does the laugh from the end of the "hold-up" exchange.)* Haaaa ha ha ha ha ha!

ERNESTO.

LISTEN TO THE TALE OF AN OUTLAW SO WISE.
WITH A FIRE IN HIS HEART AND A STORM IN HIS EYES
AND WOMAN AFTER WOMAN, THEY COME WHEN HE CALLS
TO A SHRIVELED JALAPEÑO AND TWO TINY …

GUILLERMO. *(Entering from offstage.)* OK! That's it! *(Taking Ernesto over to a chair.)* You all done for now. You sit right there, OK, and you think about what you done. I tell you when I want you to sing. *(To the pit.)* Give me a G sharp. *(They do so. Guillermo, out to the audience.)* OK … "The Ballad of Me."

WHOOOOOOOO — OOOOOOOOO
LAYS DOWN HIS LIFE FOR THE LOW AND DOWNTROD?
WHO RANSACKS THE RICH LIKE A RECKONING GOD?
WHO HIDES WITH HIS HOMBRES HIGH UP IN THE HILLS,
WHERE THE BLOOD OF THE FEDERALES HE FREQUENTLY SPILLS?

(Guillermo crosses up center where he is handed his horse, "Caballo," a broom-stick horse made up to look exactly like him. Guillermo and Ernesto together control all of Caballo's movements and sounds.) Steady there, Caballo!

I RIDE DOWN THE MOUNTAIN AT BLISTERING SPEED,
ON THE BACK OF MY TRUSTY AND LIGHTNING-FAST STEED!
AND TALES OF MY FAME SPREAD MORE QUICKLY THAN FIRE,
AND SO DO THE SKIRTS OF THE GIRLS I DESIRE!

(Pointing his gun at Ernesto.) Sing!

GUILLERMO and ERNESTO.

GUILLERMO, THE LEGEND,

GUILLERMO, THE GAME'S M.V.P.
HE'S *NUMERO UNO.*
HE'S THE MAN ALL THE MEN
IN THEIR MINDS WANT TO BE.
LET THEM DREAM OF GLORY.
WHAT HARM COULD THERE BE?
GUILLERMO.
    NO ONE DOES GLORY LIKE ME
Here ... *(Handing Caballo to Ernesto.)* you hold Caballo. And perhaps sing a
pleasing harmony.

GUILLERMO.	ERNESTO.
TONIGHT BY THE LIGHT	
OF A *MAÑANA* MOON.	OOOOOOOOOOOOOOOO
I HAVE COME TO THIS CANTINA	
WHERE MY LOVE WILL COME SOON.	OOOOOOOOOOOOOOOO
ESTA NOCHE, MY LOVE,	
THEN *MAÑANA* MY BRIDE.	OOOOOOOOOOOOOOOO ...
THEN BACK UP TO THE HILLS	
WHERE SHE FIGHTS BY MY SIDE.	

GUILLERMO and ERNESTO.
    GUILLERMO, THE LEGEND,
    GUILLERMO, THE GAME'S M.V.P.
    HE'S *NUMERO UNO*
    HE'S THE MAN ALL THE MEN
    IN THEIR MINDS WANT TO BE.
    LET THEM DREAM OF GLORY.
    WHAT HARM COULD THERE BE?
GUILLERMO. *OK,* I take it from here, *gracias.*
    'CUZ NO-O-O-O-O, NO ONE ...
    NOOOOOO NO NO NO NO, NOOOO ONE ...
    NOOOOOO NO NO,
    NO ONE DOES GLORY LIKE
    ME!
    AIY!
(The sound of a crash is heard.)
ERNESTO. *(Exiting.)* Trouble in the kitchen ...
ROSALINDA. *(Offstage.)*
    AH AH AHA AH AH AH AH AHHH
GUILLERMO. *(He sighs out to us.)* It is my love! *(Then singing to her.)*

AH AH AHA AH AH AH AH AHHH
ROSALINDA. *(Offstage.)*
AH AH AHA AH AH AH AH AHHH
GUILLERMO. Hear how she echoes my love!
AH AH AHA AH AH AH AH AHHH
(Rosalinda enters, riding another broomstick horse, made up to look exactly like her. She is the farmer's daughter and not such a big thinker.) Rosalinda!
ROSALINDA. Guillermo! *(Guillermo's horse sputters. Rosalinda's horse whinnies.)*
ROSALINDA and GUILLERMO.

COME BE MY
ALWAYS, ONLY,
EVER AFTER,
ANSWER TO MY PRAYERS.
COME BE MY LOVE.

ROSALINDA.

I COME FROM VALLEYS, WARM AND BRIGHT.

GUILLERMO.

I COME FROM HILLS SO COLD AND GREY.

ROSALINDA.

YOU COME FROM GUNS AND FEAR AND NIGHT.

GUILLERMO.

YOU COME FROM GOATS AND SHEEP AND HAY.

ROSALINDA and GUILLERMO.

TWO DIFF'RENT WORLDS ARE WE.
INTO ONE THING WE ROLL.
LOVE TAKES OUR TINY HALVES,
AND MAKES A GREAT BIG WHOLE.
COME BE MY
ALWAYS, ONLY
EVER AFTER,
ANSWER TO MY PRAYERS
COME BE MY LOVE

ROSALINDA.

I BRING A HEART THAT LONGS FOR FLIGHT

GUILLERMO.

I BRING A STRENGTH NO MAN DESTROYS.

ROSALINDA.

I BRING YOU HIPS OF PURE DELIGHT.

GUILLERMO.
    I BRING A PELVIS FULL OF JOY.
ROSALINDA and GUILLERMO.
    RING OUT THE MISSION BELLS
    TONIGHT WE SAY, "I DO."
ROSALINDA.
    MY HEART BEGINS TO SWELL.
GUILLERMO.
    I THINK I'M SWELLING TOO.
ROSALINDA and GUILLERMO.
    COME BE MY
    ALWAYS, ONLY,
    EVER AFTER
    ANSWER TO MY PRAYERS.
    COME BE MY …

(Ernesto can no longer hold himself back. He throws the horses off to each side of him and they are caught by two offstage hands. They continue to follow the action onstage.)

ERNESTO. NOOOO!!! Rosalinda, I beg you, do not do this thing. He will throw you away like all of the others. Did you not hear his ballad? Right now, I offer you my hand, as someone who has loved you with a pure heart from the first time you ever walked into my cantina.

GUILLERMO. Don't listen to the teeny man. Pick me, Rosalinda. Let me show you a passion you never thought imaginable.

ERNESTO. No, pick me, Rosalinda. Let me show you a heart that will always stay true to you!

ROSALINDA. *(Out to us.) Madre de Dios!* What am I gonna do?

GUILLERMO.
    PICK ME, ROSALINDA,
    PICK PASSION AND DESIRE.
ERNESTO.
    NO, PICK ME, ROSALINDA,
    PICK CUDDLE BY THE FIRE.
GUILLERMO.
    NO, PICK ME, ROSALINDA,
    PICK DANCING TILL THE DAWN.
ERNESTO.
    NO, PICK ME, ROSALINDA,
    PICK YOUR LONELY DAYS ARE GONE.
    THAT'S RIGHT, PICK ME, ROSALINDA,

PICK WALKING HAND-IN-HAND.
GUILLERMO.
    NO, PICK ME, ROSALINDA
    PICK DO IT IN THE SAND.
ERNESTO.
    NO, PICK ME, ROSALINDA,
    PICK KISSING YOU GOOD NIGHT
GUILLERMO.
    NO, PICK ME, ROSALINDA,
    PICK A CHOC'LATE SYRUP FIGHT.
ERNESTO and GUILLERMO.
    HEY! LISTEN TO ME, ROSALINDA,
    DEEP INSIDE YOU KNOW
    YOU'RE CHOOSING FROM YOUR HEART
    NOT EENY MEENY MINY MO!
    HEY, LISTEN, ROSALINDA,
    WE HAVE GOT TO MAKE YOU SEE
    THAT OUT OF ALL THE MEN ON EARTH,
    THE ONE YOU NEED IS ME!
GUILLERMO.
    IS ME!
ERNESTO.
    PICK ME, ROSALINDA, PICK DEEP ROMANTIC GLANCE.
GUILLERMO.
    NO, PICK ME, ROSALINDA,
    PICK PARTY IN YOUR PANTS!
ERNESTO.
    NO, PICK ME, ROSALINDA,
    PICK FINGERS THROUGH YOUR HAIR.
GUILLERMO.
    NO, PICK ME, ROSALINDA,
    PICK SOME NAUGHTY UNDERWEAR.
    THAT'S RIGHT, PICK ME, ROSALINDA,
    PICK "OH, YOU DIRTY BOY!"
ERNESTO.
    NO, PICK ME, ROSALINDA,
    PICK "MAMA'S PRIDE AND JOY."
GUILLERMO.
    NO, PICK ME, ROSALINDA,

PICK TEASE ME WITH YOUR CHARMS.

ERNESTO.

    NO, PICK ME, ROSALINDA,

    PICK JUST HOLD ME IN YOUR ARMS.

ERNESTO and GUILLERMO.

    HEY! WE CANNOT BE TOO CAREFUL

    WHEN WE'RE PLAYING FOR YOUR HEART.

ERNESTO.

    HEY, I LOVE YOU!

GUILLERMO.

    HEY, I NEED YOU!

ERNESTO and GUILLERMO.

    HEY! IT'S TEARING US APART.

    'CUZ ONE OF US WILL WIN YOU,

    AND THE OTHER ONE WILL LOSE.

    ROSALINDA, DO IT QUICK

    AND DON'T LEAVE TOO MUCH OF A BRUISE!

ERNESTO.

    PICK ME, ROSALINDA,

    PICK LOOK INTO MY EYES.

GUILLERMO.

    NO, PICK ME, ROSALINDA,

    PICK "YES, IT'S SUPER-SIZED."

ERNESTO.

    NO, PICK ME, ROSALINDA,

    PICK SWEEP YOU OFF YOUR FEET.

    NO, PICK ME, ROSALINDA,

    PICK SOME LET'S BE INDISCREET.

ERNESTO and GUILLERMO.

    RIGHT NOW! PICK ME, ROSALINDA,

    PICK "DO IT TO ME THERE!"

    NO, PICK ME, ROSALINDA,

    PICK "DON'T COME UP FOR AIR!"

    YEAH, PICK ME, ROSALINDA

    PICK, "NO, I'M STILL NOT THROUGH!"

    HEY, PICK ME, ROSALINDA,

    PICK THE THINGS I'M GONNA DO TO YOU!

    PICK ME, ROSALINDA,

    MAKE ALL MY DREAMS COME TRUE!

JUST PICK ME, ROSALINDA,
PICK ME, DO! DO!
JUST PICK ME, ROSALINDA,
PICK ME, DO! DO!

ROSALINDA. Ernesto, come here to me! *(Ernesto crosses in to Rosalinda. He kisses her passionately. Music while he does so.)* Guillermo, come here to me! *(Guillermo crosses in to Rosalinda. He kisses her with over-the-top passion. Music again, this time much more elaborate and obviously passionate. The kiss over, she turns back to Ernesto.)* Ernesto … *(She goes to him and gives him a peck on the cheek.)* Adios. *(Rosalinda and Guillermo exit on horseback. Rosalinda's horse whinnies on exiting. As Guillermo exits, his horse turns back to sputter at Ernesto.)*
ERNESTO.

SOME FLAMES BURN BRIGHTER THAN ALL OF THE REST.
BUT THAT DOESN'T PROVE THAT HIS FLAME IS THE BEST.
IT WILL SHINE OUT ITS LIGHT FOR ONE NIGHT, THEN IT'S
    THROUGH.
BUT THE FLAME THAT WILL WARM HER FOREVER
IS THE FLAME THAT IS BLUE.
HERE STANDS HER TRUE LOVE.
HERE STANDS HER BLUE FLAME.
THERE GOES MY ONLY JOY
LEAVING THIS LONELY BOY
TO BURN FOR HER.
HIS SPARKS FLY HIGHER
THEN QUICKLY TIRE.
AND SPARKS MAY DRAW A LARGER CROWD TO SEE THEM DANCE.
NOT A SOUL THERE FEELS THE REAL ROMANCE
OF BLUE.
BLUE IS THE CLEAREST SKY,
BLUE IS MY LOVER'S EYE.
BLUE IS THE WIDEST SEA
THAT'S KEEPING ME
FROM WHERE MY WISHES LIE.
BLUE IS THE BIRD OF LOVE,
BLUE IS THE MOON ABOVE.
BLUE IS THIS VALENTINE
SUNG FROM THIS HEART OF MINE.

(Solo break as Ernesto begins to clean up the restaurant. Lights up on Kitty. She is from our last restaurant, the Star-Lite Diner. She is reading a romance novel entitled

41

The Blue Flame. *She reads to us as Ernesto works.)*
KITTY.   "As Ernesto watched Rosalinda ride off into the moonlight with Guillermo, he felt, in the recesses of his breaking heart, a swift and sudden breeze which threatened to extinguish the light of his love. The only thing he knew to do was to protect that flickering flame, to tend to its embers, in case Rosalinda ever chanced to return to the warmth of its light."
ERNESTO.
> I WILL STILL BE TRUE.
> WHAT MORE CAN I DO?
> I WILL STOKE THIS FIRE
> WITH PURE DESIRE
> AND LOVE FOR YOU.
> I WILL CALL YOUR NAME
> UNTIL YOU SEE THIS FLAME.
> WHEN HIS LOVE DISAPPEARS
> I WILL BE WAITING HERE.

ERNESTO and KITTY.
> FOR I'M YOUR TRUE LOVE.
> I AM YOUR BLUE FLAME.
> AND THOUGH MY LIGHT IS SMALL,
> MY HEAT IS ALL
> THE WARMTH YOU'LL EVER NEED.
> PLEASE FIND YOUR TRUE LOVE.
> PLEASE FIND YOUR BLUE FLAME.
> AND MAY IT START A FIRE DOWN INSIDE YOU TOO
> THAT BURNS AS DEEPLY AS MY FLAME OF BLUE

ERNESTO.
> FOR YOU.

(Ernesto exits. Kitty closes the book and sighs deeply. Music begins.)
KITTY.   Tonight, I follow your example, Ernesto. Tonight, I reveal my blue flame to my secret love. If there's anyone up there looking down on me, please, look down kindly and wish me luck! *(She crosses back to the table, as Clutch enters, the object of her desire. He is dancing, combing his hair and holding a note written on very feminine stationary. The stereotypical rebel/car mechanic low on brains, he sings out to us.)*
CLUTCH.
> SOMEONE LEFT THIS NOTE
> ON MY WINDSHIELD TODAY,
> AND EV'RY INCH WAS COVER'D
> WITH SOME PERFUME SPRAY.

IT SAID, "I'M FALLING FOR YOU, BABY,
WITH ALL OF MY MIGHT!
WHY DON'T YOU MEET ME AT THE
STAR-LITE DINER TONIGHT?"

KITTY. Hi, Clutch.

CLUTCH. *(Barely noticing her.)* Oh hi, Kitty.

WELL, ALL THE INK WAS PINK
THE "I"'S WERE DOTTED WITH HEARTS.
AND THE WORDS GOT PRETTY TRICKY
IN A COUPLE OF PARTS.
BUT THE LITTLE THAT I GOT
MADE SOME FEELINGS IGNITE!
THERE MIGHT BE TRUE LOVE
BREWING AT THE STAR-LITE TONIGHT.

KITTY.

THERE MIGHT BE TRUE LOVE
BREWING AT THE STAR-LITE TONIGHT!

Hey Clutch, whatchya got there?

CLUTCH. It's a note from a girl. A mystery girl.

KITTY. A *MYSTERY* girl? What does *THAT* mean?

CLUTCH. She's a mystery. She didn't sign her name or anything. She just told me to meet her here at the Star-Lite tonight.

KITTY. Well Clutch, how will you know who she is?

CLUTCH. Gee Kitty, I didn't think of that. *(Lightbulb.)* Wait a minute! She says what she looks like right here in the note.

KITTY. Really, Clutch? What does she say? *(Clutch sings the complete description of what Kitty is wearing.)*

CLUTCH.

SHE'LL WEAR A PAIR PEDAL PUSHERS
AND HER BLOUSE WILL BE BLUE.
SHE'LL HAVE A SWEATER IF IT'S CHILLY,
AND A NECKERCHIEF TOO.
A PAIR OF CAT'S-EYE GLASSES,
AND HER HAIR PULLED BACK TIGHT.
THAT'S HOW I'LL KNOW SHE'S AT
THE STAR-LITE DINER TONIGHT.

KITTY. Wow Clutch, a real live *MYSTERY DATE!!!*

CLUTCH.

'CUZ I'VE BEEN WAITIN'

KITTY.

    I'VE BEEN WAITIN'

CLUTCH.

    FOR A LOVE THAT IS TRUE.

    I'M SICK OF DATIN'

KITTY.

    SICK OF DATIN'

CLUTCH.

    GIRLS WHO DON'T HAVE A CLUE.

    SO IF CUPID SHOOTS HIS ARROW

    AND IT HITS HER JUST RIGHT,

    THERE MIGHT BE TRUE LOVE

    BREWING AT THE STAR-LITE TONIGHT.

KITTY.

    THERE MIGHT BE TRUE LOVE

    BREWING AT THE STAR-LITE TONIGHT!

KITTY and CLUTCH.

    TRUE LOVE AT THE STAR-LITE DINER

    WITH THE BIRDS AND THE BEES AND NOTHIN' COULD BE
        FINER.

    TRUE LOVE WHILE WE TWIST AND SHOUT,

    PUMPING NICKELS IN THE JUKEBOX TILL WE DANCE EACH
        OTHER OUT.

    TRUE LOVE, LET IT START TONIGHT

    WITH A HUG AND A KISS AND A-HOLD EACH OTHER TIGHT.

    TRUE LOVE ON MY MYST'RY DATE!

    I'VE BEEN DREAMING (HER/HIM.) FOREVER,

    HOW MUCH LONGER MUST I WAIT?

(Pops enters. He's the owner/manager of the Star-Lite Diner, and the nearest father-figure his clientele has. He is perpetually drying off a tin milk shake cup with a dish towel.)

POPS. What are you kids going on about out here?

KITTY and CLUTCH. Oh, hi Pops.

KITTY. Clutch is on a date with a *MYSTERY* girl.

POPS. A *MYSTERY* girl? What's that?

CLUTCH. Can't talk right now, Pops. I've gotta be on the lookout for her.

POPS. Well, you be careful, Clutch. Going around, breaking these girls' hearts. When are you gonna settle down, Clutch?

CLUTCH. Maybe tonight, Pops. Maybe tonight I find my true love.

    MAYBE AFTER ALL THE GIRLS

I'VE DATED BEFORE
THERE'S AN ANGEL SENT FROM HEAVEN
HEADING RIGHT TO MY DOOR.
I CAN FEEL HER HERE BESIDE ME.
IF I PLAY MY CARDS RIGHT
THERE MIGHT BE TRUE LOVE
BREWING AT THE STAR-LITE TONIGHT.
KITTY and POPS.
   THERE MIGHT BE TRUE LOVE
   BREWING AT THE STAR-LITE TONIGHT!

CLUTCH.	KITTY and POPS.
SO TWINKLE, TWINKLE	
	TWINKLE, TWINKLE
LITTLE STAR WAY UP HIGH.	LITTLE STAR
I'M ASKING SWEETLY	
	ASKING SWEETLY
AS I LOOK TO THE SKY.	FROM WHERE YOU ARE.
SHINE SOME TWINKLE DOWN	
ON ME,	AHHH, AHHH
SEND ME HEAVENLY LIGHT.	AHHH, AHHH
BRING ME SOME TRUE LOVE	
BREWING AT THE STAR-LITE	
TONIGHT.	

CLUTCH, KITTY and POPS.
   TRUE LOVE AT THE STAR-LITE

CLUTCH.	KITTY and POPS.
THE STAR-LITE TONIGHT!	TRUE LOVE
	BREWING AT THE STAR-LITE TONIGHT.
	TRUE LOVE
	BREWING AT THE STAR-LITE TONIGHT.

CLUTCH, KITTY and POPS.
   TRUE LOVE AT THE STAR-LITE TONIGHT.
(*A huge kitchen crash that goes on and on and on. At the end of it, Pops looks out at the audience and conducts them in the line reading of …)*
AUDIENCE. Trouble in the kitchen!!!
POPS. (*Exiting.*) What *they* said!
CLUTCH. I'm gonna go check the parking lot. She coulda shown up while we were singing. (*Exit.*)
KITTY. (*Chasing after him.*) But Clutch, wait … *I'm* your "mystery … girl."

45

LIKE A PUZZLE, WITH ONE PIECE THAT'S GONE ASTRAY.
LIKE A DOOR WITH NO KEY.
JUST LIKE NIGHTFALL IN THE MIDDLE OF THE DAY.
THAT'S THE MYST'RY THAT LOVE IS TO ME.

(Clutch reenters.)

CLUTCH. Say, Kitty … I was out in the parking lot, and I thought to myself, "WAIT a minute. What about Kitty?" *(Kitty crosses to Clutch. Clutch takes her hand, clears his throat …)* Kitty, have YOU seen anyone who looks like this? *(Note from the pit, Clutch buries his face in the note again, looking for clues. Kitty turns out to us.)*

KITTY.	CLUTCH.
IT'S A MYST'RY HE SEES NOTHING IN THESE EYES.	WHAT ARE "CAT'S-EYE" GLASSES?
IT'S A MYST'RY TO ME THAT ONLY I KNOW HOW OFTEN I CRY OVER A LOVE THAT WILL NOT BE.	ARE THEY JUST GLASSES MADE FOR CATS?
IT'S A MYST'RY	IT'S A MYST'RY
	THAT SHE'D LEAVE THIS NOTE BEHIND AND HIDE HER LOVE SO FAR AWAY.
TEN LITTLE FEET AWAY FROM YOU	
	SHE'S PLAYING "HARD TO GET" AND IT'S DRIVING ME OUT OF MY MIND. BABY, COME OUT NOW AND PLAY.
AND I'M FRESH OUT OF HOPE.	I'M AT THE END OF MY ROPE
AND BELIEVE ME IT'S A LONG, LONG WAY TO FALL.	AND BELIEVE ME IT'S A LONG, LONG WAY TO LONG, LONG WAY TO FALL.
	I HAVE SEARCHED FROM TOP TO BOTTOM
YOU WANT HEARTACHES, FOLKS, I'VE GOT 'EM.	
	I AM A FOOL FOR HER LOVE
I WANT HEAVEN ABOVE TO SOLVE THIS MYST'RY	
	SOLVE THE MYST'RY

46

KITTY.	CLUTCH.
	OF MY MYST'RY GIRL AND ME.
IT'S ME, IT'S ME, IT'S ME …	
	PLEASE BE A MYST'RY NO MORE.
MORE, MORE, MORE, MORE …	
	STEP OUT OF THE SHADOWS NOW
	AND BABY, LET ME SEE
JUST WHAT MY HEART'S	JUST WHAT MY HEART'S
BEEN WAITING FOR.	BEEN WAITING FOR.
	IT'S GETTING AWFULLY LATE
ON THIS MYSTERY DATE	
AND IT LOOKS LIKE	AND IT LOOKS LIKE
LOVE IS PASSING ME,	LOVE IS PASSING ME BY.
PASSING ME BY.	
AND I'LL CRY MYSELF	
TO SLEEP NOW.	
	ONLY A NOTE FOR ME TO KEEP NOW.
I ASK THE STARS IN THE SKY.	
CAN YOU PLEASE TELL ME?	CAN YOU PLEASE TELL ME?
WHY DOES HE	WHY DOES SHE
LOOK THE OTHER WAY …	LOOK THE OTHER WAY …
WHEN I AM STANDING	
RIGHT HERE?	
	HERE IS MY HEART, NOW WHERE ARE YOU?
HIS LOVE IS SEARCHING STILL	
BUT MINE IS HERE TO STAY.	
IS IT A MYST'RY	
	YOU'RE STILL A MYST'RY …
THAT I END UP	
	HOW WILL THIS END UP?
IN TEARS?	
	TEARS IN MY HEART
	'CUZ IT'S BROKEN APART OVER …

KITTY. If I see her, Clutch, you'll be the first to know.

CLUTCH. Thanks, Kitty. You're the best. (*He exits. Music starts. Pops enters, dish rag and frappe tin in hand. He sings out to us about Kitty's failed "mystery date" plan.*)

POPS. Look at her, poor kid. Wouldn't know the real thing if it smacked her right between the eyes …

   SHE'S LOOKING FOR LOVE

IN THE STORIES SHE READS.
BUT A FICTIONAL FLING
ISN'T WHAT THIS GIRL NEEDS.
And listen to some of these books she's been reading ... *(Chord from band as he holds up a book.)*
DALLYIN' WITH MY ITALIAN STALLION
(He turns it to read the description on the back cover.) "Married to a mobster, but flirting with disaster." Or ... *(Chord from band as he holds up another book.)*
MEINE VERBOTENE DREI-HENDIGE LIEBE
(He turns it to read the description on the back cover.) Which, translated, means "My forbidden three-handed love." Or my personal favorite ... *(A final chord from band as he holds up another book.)* ... The Blue Flame, *(He turns it to read the description on the back cover.)*
"A PASSIONATE BATTLE BETWEEN LUST AND LOVE."
It's *muy caliente!*
TRUMPED UP AFFAIRS
IN SOME DIME-STORE ROMANCE
WITH HER EYES IN A BOOK,
TRUE LOVE DON'T STAND A CHANCE
(Magical music and lights which Kitty reacts to, then Gino appears.)
GINO. Hey, Kitty ... What gives? ... You're not yourself tonight.
THE WAY I'M WRITTEN
WOMEN ARE SMITTEN.
I FILL THEIR HEADS WITH LUST
UNTIL I GAIN THEIR TRUST.
THAT'S HOW I PLAY.
AFTER THEY GIVE THEIR HEART
I RIP THEIR LIVES APART.
WHAT CAN I SAY?
Wake up, Kitty!!!
WERE YOU BORN YESTERDAY?
TRUE LOVE DON'T HAPPEN THAT WAY.
(Gino exits, and Heimlich enters from the German restaurant.)
HEIMLICH.
TO THINK THAT YOU WOULD CHOOSE REGRET,
INSTEAD OF OPENING YOURSELF TO LOVE ...
THIS IS A PAIN NOT WORTH THE BEARING.
INSTEAD OF READING OTHER PEOPLE'S HEARTS,
PERHAPS IT'S TIME TO LOOK INTO YOUR OWN.

PUT DOWN THE BOOK, GO OUT, UND RISK LOVE.
RISK LOVE …
Bitte …
RISK LOVE!
(Heimlich exits, and Guillermo enters from the Mexican restaurant.)
GUILLERMO.
BLUE FLAME OR WHITE FLAME, WHO CARES HOW IT LOOKS!
'CUZ YOU CAN'T FEEL THE HEAT WHEN IT'S STUCK IN A BOOK!
YOU CAN READ ABOUT LOVE, YOU CAN DREAM OF IT TOO!
IT'S A TOTALLY DIFFERENT FEELING …
WHEN LOVE LOOKS BACK AT YOU!
WHEN LOVE LOOKS BACK … AT YOU!
KITTY.
I KNOW THAT WHEN I READ
I'M JUST PRETENDING
BUT CUPID, IT'S THE ONLY WAY
I'LL GET MY HAPPY ENDING
(Spoken.) Just look at me …
IS THERE ANY CHANCE
I'LL EVER FIND A REAL ROMANCE
WILL I NEVER SEE
LOVE LOOKING BACK AT ME …
POPS. Say Kitty, would you mind taking the graveyard shift? I've got a little errand I'd like to run.
KITTY. Sure thing, Pops. See you tomorrow.
I AM THROUGH WITH LOVE.
I'M THROUGH WITH ENDING UP THIS WAY.
THE FINAL CHAPTER AND I'M STILL HERE ALONE.
COVER TO COVER, AND NO MAN OF MY OWN.
CUPID MUST HAVE BETTER THINGS TO DO
THAN WASTE HIS TIME ON FOOLS LIKE ME.
I'VE READ SO MANY WORDS OF LOVE,
BUT NONE GIVE ME THE FEELING OF
A LOVE THAT'S LOOKING BACK AT ME.
'CUZ NOT A ONE OF US
WAS MEANT TO WALK THIS ROAD ALONE.
STILL I KEEP PRAYING UP AROUND THE NEXT BEND
THAT SOMEONE WATCHING OVER ME HAS CHOSEN TO SEND
THE ONE THAT I'VE BEEN DREAMING OF

THE ONE WHO'LL LOOK INTO THESE EYES
AND SEE WHAT HE'S BEEN WAITING FOR,
AND TAKE BACK ALL THOSE NIGHTS BEFORE,
WHEN LOVE WOULD NOT LOOK BACK AT ME.

(Matt enters the diner. Pops meets him at the "door.")

MATT. One, please.

POPS. Right this way. *(Pops walks Matt over to the table. Matt sits and Pops exits and returns with a menu for him.)*

KITTY.
WHEN WILL I SEE LOVE
LOOKING BACK AT ME?

POPS. Long night?

MATT. Mmm-hmmm.

KITTY.
I'VE BEEN WAITING HERE PATIENTLY
CAN YOU PLEASE FIND YOUR WAY

(Pops hands Matt the menu.)

POPS. By the by, try the Number Four. *(Pops exits.)*

KITTY.
SOMEONE UP ABOVE
REACH DOWN GENTLY AND GUIDE MY LOVE
I'VE BEEN HOPING SO LONG THAT LOVE WOULD LOOK BACK
AT ME …

MATT.
I'M A VERY SINGLE MAN.
I'M TELLING YOU, A VERY SINGLE MAN.
AND I'M THROUGH WITH BEING LOVE'S MISTAKE.
I'M DONE WITH ENDING UP THIS WAY.
I MAKE IT THROUGH ANOTHER TERRIBLE NIGHT
AND A VOICE DOWN DEEP INSIDE ME SAYS, "DON'T GIVE UP
   THE FIGHT."

MATT.	KITTY.
WHAT I'D GIVE TO BE THE LUCKY ONE.	WHAT I'D GIVE TO BE THE LUCKY ONE.
WHAT I'D GIVE TO KNOW SHE'S LOOKING NOW.	
	WHAT I'D GIVE.

MATT and KITTY.
TO SEE MYSELF INSIDE THOSE EYES,

AND JUST LIKE THAT TO REALIZE
MATT.
    THAT LOVE IS LOOKING BACK AT ME.
KITTY.
    THAT LOVE IS LOOKING BACK AT ME.
MATT.
    PLEASE LOVE, LOOK BACK AT ME.
KITTY.
    PLEASE LOVE, LOOK BACK.
MATT and KITTY.
    WHEN WILL I SEE LOVE
(Pops returns with "cupid wings" and sets the stage for love.)
    LOOKING BACK AT ME?
    I'VE BEEN WAITING HERE PATIENTLY.
    CAN YOU PLEASE FIND YOUR WAY?
(Kitty crosses to Matt, focused on her pad of order slips and a pencil. Matt is focused in the menu.)
    SOMEONE UP ABOVE,
    REACH DOWN GENTLY AND GUIDE MY LOVE.
    I'VE BEEN HOPING SO LONG
    THAT LOVE WOULD LOOK BACK AT …
(Matt and Kitty look at each other.)
MATT. Hi …
KITTY. Hi …
MATT.
    WHERE YOU'VE BEEN HIDING
    HELL, I HAVEN'T A CLUE.
    BUT WOULD YOU MIND STANDING THERE
    FOR THE REST OF MY DAYS?
KITTY.
    AS LONG AS STANDING HERE MEANS STANDING WITH YOU
MATT and KITTY.
    'CUZ MY HEART STARTS TO POUND
    WHEN I LOOK IN YOUR EYES,
    AND MY FEET LEAVE THE GROUND,
    AND MY TEMP'RATURE RISES.
    THE FEELING'S SO STRONG,
    I CAN'T HOLD BACK THE KISSES.
    I'VE WAITED SO LONG

AND NOW FINALLY THIS IS

MATT.	KITTY.
LOVE	THIS IS LOVE
LOVE LOOKING BACK AT ME.	LOOKING BACK AT ME.
IT TOOK AN ETERNITY	IT TOOK FOREVER
BUT YOU FOUND YOUR WAY.	FOR LOVE TO BRING YOU HERE TO ME.
SOMEONE UP ABOVE	SOMEONE WATCHING OVER
FINALLY FOUND MY LOVE.	FOUND MY LOVE.
AND I WAITED SO LONG,	I'VE BEEN WAITING.
AND I WANT IT SO MUCH.	
AND I DREAM YOU EACH NIGHT,	I'VE BEEN DREAMING.
AND I LONG FOR YOUR TOUCH.	
AFTER SUCH A LONG ROAD,	
HERE'S LOVE …	HERE'S LOVE …
LOOKING BACK AT ME!	LOOKING BACK AT ME!

(Blackout.)

End of Play

PROPERTY LIST

Flowers
Breath spray
Menus
Drinks
Paper
Money
Cell phone
Phone
Gun
Purse
Panties
Bag of money
Broomstick horses
Books
Note
Milkshake tin, dish towel
Pad, pen

SOUND EFFECTS

Bleep
Cell phones
Horns
Car horn
Five different crashes, each one bigger than the one before, the last one
     comically long
Gunshot
Thunder